A-Z Amazing Animals of the Amazon Rainforest of South America

By Mindy Sawyer

TABLE OF CONTENTS

Front and back cover pictures are the Iguazu Falls in South America

A-Z Amazing Animals of the Amazon Rainforest of South America is a fun book for ALL ages! Learn about a bird that has an **umbrella** on its head and another bird that smells like **manure**! How about a lizard with **three eyes** or a giant female rodent that **whistles through her nose** to call her boyfriend? Learn fun and interesting facts about the **world's heaviest snake, largest rodent, loudest land animal,** and a **fish** that can **bark**! These amazing animals, and many more, are in this fun and entertaining book!

FUN FOR ALL AGES:
1. **Older children** will have fun learning unusual facts about animals.
2. **Younger children:** Adults can read to younger children who are not yet reading and **both** will learn surprising facts about Amazon animals.
3. **Toddlers** will delight in the vibrant, colorful, animal photographs as they learn the animal names.
4. **Beginning Readers:** Children who are **beginning readers** can enjoy taking turns reading with an adult, as this is a *K-2 "We Can Both Read"* book! (Adults introduce the animal's name and read the blue text while budding readers read the red text with a little help until mastered.)

There is also an **INDEX** to easily locate specific animals, and a **GLOSSARY** with word definitions. This is a *fascinating and fun* educational book that will be treasured and enjoyed for years to come!

Hi! I am a *toco toucan*, the largest of the **toucans**!

Adults can read this book to a child, <u>**OR,**</u> if a child is a beginning reader, <u>the adult **first** introduces the animal's name at the start of the page</u>. Then, the child reads the words in **red.** The adult then reads the remaining words in **blue.**

(Child reads) I am a **toucan**. Do you like to eat fruit? I love to eat fruit! I also eat seeds, eggs and yummy bugs! Do you like to eat bugs? I do not fly very far, but I can hop and fly a little from tree to tree.

(Adult reads) My beak is **huge**, but it is not very heavy. It is made of keratin – the same protein that your hair and nails are made from. I use my bill to gather and peel fruit, and a large bill can attract me a cute girl toucan!

Okay, let's get started with 'A-Z Amazing Animals!' First is - A - Anaconda! →

Aa   Anaconda

Can you find this snake's eyes? It is an **anaconda snake** and it is **big!** It can swim in the water and go on land.

This is a **green anaconda snake.** It is the heaviest snake in the world and it can weigh over 550 pounds! (227 kilograms) Its green color helps it blend in and hide among leaves of the rainforest, so it is **camouflaged.** It is a constrictor, so it is not poisonous, but it constricts or squeezes its prey. The **green anaconda** eats fish, rodents, wild pigs, small deer and even caiman and jaguars!

Bb   Butterfly

A **butterfly** can be many pretty colors. It can live 2 or 3 weeks as a **butterfly** if it is lucky, as some animals want to eat it such as birds, lizards and frogs.

This butterfly is a **blue morpho butterfly**. It drinks nectar from flowers. To become an adult butterfly a butterfly must go through a big change called a **complete metamorphosis**. This big change has four stages:
1.   egg,   2. caterpillar (larva),   3. chrysalis (pupa)   and   4. adult butterfly.

Cc Capybara

Capybaras have webbed feet and are good swimmers. They have 4 toes on each front foot and 3 toes on each back foot. **Capybaras** live near water in groups that can have 10 to 20 members, but, can also get up to 100!

Capybaras are the world's largest rodents! Rodents are animals such as mice, rats and hamsters. A mouse is so small you could hold it in your hand, but a capybara can weigh 146 pounds, (66 kg) or as much as many adult humans. Capybaras are **herbivores** and eat plants, fruit and tree bark. When the female capybara wants a mate or boyfriend she will **whistle through her nose!**

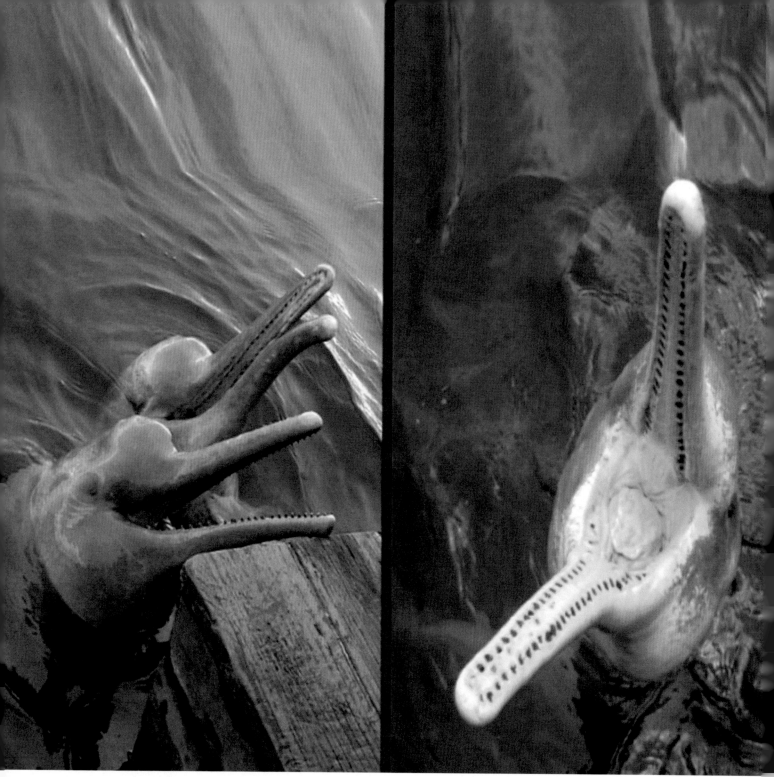

Dd   Dolphin

Dolphins are mammals and they are very smart. These are **pink river dolphins.** They are also called **Amazon river dolphins.**

Pink river dolphins are the largest fresh water dolphins in the world! Dolphins use **echolocation**, or *sound waves* in the water, to navigate and find food. They have teeth and can eat turtles and crabs. They especially like fish and even eat piranhas!

Ee Egret

An **egret** is a bird that likes to hang-out in and near water. The **great egret** eats fish, frogs, reptiles and small mammals. Both the mom and dad egret help take care of their 3 to 4 eggs.

The **great egret** was once hunted for it's pretty feathers and its population dropped by 95 percent, so it was in danger of becoming **extinct!** However, it is now protected, and its population has increased. It is the symbol of the **National Audubon Society** ® a society that protects birds and other creatures.

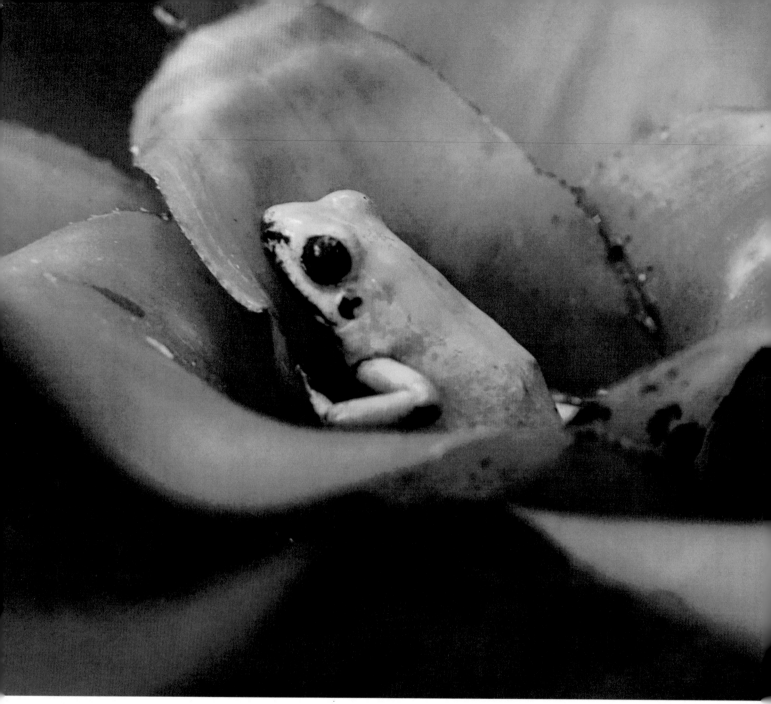

Ff Frog

This **frog** is the **golden dart frog.** It eats insects with its long, sticky tongue.

The **golden dart frog** is only about 2 inches long (50 mm) but it is one of the **most** poisonous frogs in the world! It is also known as the **golden poison arrow frog** or the **golden poison frog**.

Many poison frogs have bright colors that are a warning to other animals, **"Don't eat me! I am dangerous!"** Some frog's poison is used by native Amazon people on their arrows or darts to hunt animals.

Gg Goliath Spider

The **goliath spider** has 8 eyes, but it does not see very well. It lives in a hole in a tree, or a hole in the ground.

The **goliath spider** is a tarantula and it is the heaviest spider in the world! It is also called the **goliath birdeater** and the **goliath bird-eating tarantula**. It **can** eat birds, but, mostly it eats insects, spiders and small creatures like frogs, bats, mice, snakes and lizards. Some people in South America cook and eat the **goliath tarantula**! They say it tastes like smoky shrimp!

Hh Howler Monkeys

Howler monkeys may be brown, black or red. They mostly eat leaves, nuts, fruits and flowers.

If you ever spend the night in a rainforest you will likely hear **howler monkeys**! They are considered the loudest animals on land and their loud whooping roar can be heard from three miles away! They can use their long prehensile (gripping) tail like an extra hand and even use it to hang upside down!

Ii Iguana Lizard

Most **iguanas** live in trees and are very good swimmers. **Iguanas** eat plants, fruits and flowers.

This is a **green iguana lizard**. It has four clever ways to protect itself from predators:
1. Its green color acts as **camouflage** and helps it blend in and hide among leaves.
2. If an animal attacks, the green iguana can jump in water and swim away.
3. A green iguana has a **_third eye_** on top of its head! It is not like a normal eye, but it can help the iguana detect movement if a predator is sneaking up on it.
4. If a predator grabs the green iguana's tail, the tail can break off! This gives the iguana a chance to escape. Even more amazing, the green iguana can **grow a new tail!**

Jj Jaguar

Jaguars are the third largest wild cat in the world. Most **jaguars** have a yellow coat with black rings, but some are all black or all white.

A **jaguar** is good at swimming and climbing. A jaguar is a carnivore. A carnivore eats other animals. A jaguar can catch and eat fish, reptiles, deer, caiman, and other animals. It is the king of the rainforest, and an apex predator at the top of the food chain. This means there are not many animals that hunt the jaguar.

Kk Kinkajou –

A **kinkajou** has a long tail like a monkey, but it is not a monkey. It has big eyes and small ears.

The **kinkajou** can hang upside down using its long, prehensile (gripping) tail. It lives in trees and its favorite food is fruit. It can use its long tongue to remove nectar from flowers or honey from bee hives! **Neat trick**: A kinkajou can turn its feet backwards and run easily in either direction on a tree branch!

Ll Leafcutter Ants

A leafcutter ant works hard! This ant can carry a leaf that is much bigger than it is, so it is very strong! It can cut a leaf very fast!

Leafcutter ants have strong jaws that can move 1,000 times per second! They take the leaves back to a hole in the ground that is their nest. The leaves will be used as food. With millions of ants carrying leaves back to their nest it can look like the forest floor is moving!

Mm Macaw Parrots

Macaw parrots sleep in trees at night and are awake and active during the day. They eat nuts, seeds, insects and fruit. They can be many different, pretty colors.

This is a **hyacinth macaw** and it is the largest parrot in the world! It is *endangered* due to habitat loss and cage bird trade. **Endangered** means there are not very many of them left in the wild, so they are in danger of becoming extinct. A **hyacinth macaw** has a very strong beak! Its strong beak can even crack hard nuts like macadamia nuts and Brazil nuts!

Nn Nutria

A **nutria** has webbed back feet and it is a good swimmer. It can hold its breath under water for up to five minutes!

A **nutria** is a big rodent. Rats and mice are also rodents, but they are much smaller. A **nutria** is also called a **coypu** or a **river rat**. It is an omnivore so it eats plants and animals, which can include aquatic plants, roots, mussels, insects and snails.

Oo   Otters

Otters like to play on land and in the water! Otters have webbed feet and are very good swimmers.

This is a picture of two **giant otters**. Giant otters are the longest otters in the world! They can be over six feet (2.5 meters) long. They eat river creatures such as snakes, crabs, turtles, small caiman, and fish such as catfish and piranhas. Giant otters are **endangered** as there are only a few thousand left in the wild.

Pp Piranhas

Piranhas are fish that have strong jaws and sharp teeth. **Piranhas** hunt in groups called schools.

Most **piranhas** are omnivores so they eat plants and animals. They eat plants, insects, worms, shellfish and fish. Native (indigenous) people of South America sometimes use the piranhas' strong jaws and sharp teeth to make tools. **The red-bellied piranhas** shown in this picture will sometimes make barking sounds if they feel threatened!

Qq Quail-Dove

Quail-doves are birds that live where there are a lot of trees. Many birds live high in the trees, but, **quail-doves** often make their nest on the ground or in a bush. They most often eat seeds and fruit on the ground.

Quail-doves are related to pigeons and doves, but, have a round body like a quail. There are different types and colors of quail-doves. This is a picture of a **violaceous quail-dove**.

Rr Red-Eyed Tree Frog

   This is a **red-eyed tree frog.** It has sticky toes that help it stick when it jumps from tree to tree.

   The **red-eyed tree frog** is an **amphibian** so it spends part of its life in water and part on land. The clever female red-eyed tree frog lays her eggs on a leaf that hangs over water, so that when the baby tadpoles hatch from the eggs, they fall into the water. Tadpoles are good swimmers. They eat small insects and eventually grow into froglets and then into adult frogs.

Ss Stinkbird

A baby **stinkbird** has claws on its wings! It can use its claws, beak and toes to climb trees! As it gets older, and begins to fly, the wing claws get smaller. If a baby **stinkbird** falls in the water it can swim, but, its parents cannot swim.

A **stinkbird** is also called a **hoatzin**. It is one of the strangest birds in the Amazon rainforest! It looks like a chicken with a small head and it is rather clumsy when it flies. It is called a **stinkbird** because it smells like manure! It is sometimes called a 'flying cow' because, like a cow, it has more than one stomach. It is believed that the stinkbird's unusual smell is caused by rotting leaves and fruit in its stomach.

Tt Tapir

A tapir has 4 toes on each front foot and 3 toes on each back foot. A tapir spends a lot of time in the water and it is a very good swimmer. If a tapir gets scared it can hide under water and stick its trunk above the water to get air.

A tapir looks like a pig with a short trunk, but it is related to horses and rhinos. A tapir has a short prehensile (gripping) trunk, which is an extended nose and upper lip. They use this trunk to grab leaves, plants or tasty fruit. A female tapir will be pregnant for 13 months. She usually gives birth to one baby. The baby is called a calf and it can stand up a couple of hours after being born.

Uu Umbrellabird

An **umbrellabird** eats frogs, lizards, insects and spiders. The female will lay one or more eggs. She takes care of the eggs and baby chicks by herself.

When it's looking for a mate the male **umbrellabird** will fan out his *crest* (head feathers) like an umbrella to show-off for the ladies! This is a picture of a **long-wattled umbrellabird.** A wattle is extra skin that hangs down onto its chest. The male umbrella bird uses his wattle to make a loud, flute-like noise in the morning and evening.

Vv   Vampire Bat

Bats are the only mammals that can fly. Besides flying, **vampire bats** can also run, walk, and hop like a bunny!

Vampire bats drink blood from other animals to survive. (This does not usually hurt the other animals.) Vampire bats are nocturnal so they are awake at night and sleep during the day, hanging upside down, in caves or trees. They use echolocation (sound waves) to navigate when they fly at night.

Ww Woolly Monkey

The **woolly monkey** has a lot of fur! Its fur coat helps protect it from the rain, sun, and insect bites or stings.

The **woolly monkey** is an omnivore which means it eats both meat and plants. Its favorite food is fruit. It has a prehensile (gripping) tail that helps it grip onto branches and climb more easily.

Xx X-Ray Tetra Fish

The **X-ray tetra fish** eats worms and insects. It is small and only about 2 inches (5 cm) long. It lives in big groups called schools.

The **X-ray tetra fish** has a *transparent* body – that means you can see through its clear skin and see its backbone inside its body! Scientists think its transparent skin may protect it from predators as it may be harder to see the tetra swimming in shimmering water.

Yy Yapok

A **yapok** has webbed back feet so it is a very good swimmer. It eats fish, frogs and other water animals.

A **yapok** is also called a **water opossum.** It has waterproof fur and builds its den underground, in a river bank. It is the only living marsupial where both the male and female have pouches! (With other marsupials only the female will have a pouch and she uses it to carry her baby.)

<u>Zz Zorro Short-eared dog</u>

The **zorro** mostly eats fish, but, also eats insects, birds, crabs, frogs, reptiles, small mammals and fruit.

Although **zorro** means 'fox' in Spanish, the **zorro** is actually a member of the dog family, not the fox family. The zorro is also called the **short-eared zorro** and **small-eared dog**. It has short, round ears and a bushy tail. It is mostly nocturnal or active at night. It lives near water and its paws are partly webbed!

Thanks for reading! This is the first book in a series that will be coming soon! Mindy Sawyer is writing another book and we will be learning more fun facts about animals from around the world!

Also, you can check-out a funny book Mindy wrote called **"Gabby Meets Vlad the Vampire."** It's on Amazon.com as a Kindle or a paperback. **Have fun reading!**

 **Love,
Mr. Monkey
Jan. 2017**

DEDICATION:

This book is dedicated to my brother, Mike, who makes me laugh and has a heart of gold, and to my sister, Becky, who is a sweet, funny, beautiful spirit. Love you both to the moon and stars and back! Also, a special thanks to my sweet Granddaughter, Destinee, for listening to my ideas and for being the incredible smart, funny and special young lady that you are!

Fun websites for kids with additional animal information and games
http://kids.nationalgeographic.com/videos/
http://www.nwf.org/kids/ranger-rick/animals.aspx
http://pbskids.org/wildkratts/
http://www.sciencekids.co.nz/sciencefacts/animals.html
http://www.softschools.com/facts/animals/

INDEX/PAGE

GLOSSARY

Amphibian – an animal that starts life in water and later can move to land.

Bird – An egg laying animal with wings and feathers.

Camouflage – a pattern or color that matches an animal's surroundings and helps it hide and blend in.

Carnivore – a meat eater

Echolocation - locating things by bouncing sound waves off of them.

Endangered – animals at risk of becoming extinct

Herbivore – a plant eater

Mammal – an animal that gives birth to live young, has hair or fur and feeds its young milk.

Marsupial – a mammal with a pouch used to carry its young

Metamorphosis – when an animal transforms and has a major change in its appearance

Nectar – the sweet liquid inside flowers

Nocturnal – awake and active at night

Omnivore – an animal that eats plants and meat

Predator – an animal that hunts and eats other animals.

Prehensile tail – a tail that can grip and hold like a hand.

Prey – an animal hunted for food.

Reptile – an animal that has scales, is cold-blooded and lays eggs.

Rodent – a mammal that has 4 gnawing or nibbling front teeth

Transparent – clear enough to see through

45069142R00019

Made in the USA
San Bernardino, CA
30 January 2017